THE ULTIMATE GUIDE TO

PICKING A PERFECT

PHOTO BOOTH

MARTIN L. SMITH

Lemby Publishing
2232 S. Main St. #216
Ann Arbor, MI 48103

Ordering Information:
Special discounts are available on quantity purchases by corporations, associations, and others. For details, contact the "Special Sales Department" at the address above.

The Ultimate Guide To Picking a Perfect Photo Booth
Martin L. Smith. -- 1st ed.
ISBN 978-0692361863

DEDICATION

This book is dedicated to our entire staff and every client who's worked with us at PhotoBoothPlus.com. The last 6 years have been a wonderful journey, and I thank you for your dedication and patronage, which has directly led to the publishing of this book. May God bless each of you!

INTRODUCTION

You cracked the cover of this book. That means you're likely researching a photo booth for your wedding, party, corporate event, or other special occasion. Even if you don't have the foggiest clue about what to look for or how to compare, this book will show you everything you need to know to choose the right booth and get it at the best possible cost.

The highest priced photo booth won't necessarily deliver the highest quality, and the lowest priced booth may cut corners or use deceptive practices that cost you more in the long run. Knowing basic information about photo booth rentals will make sure you reserve a booth at a price that fits your budget, while getting the quality you deserve.

My goal here is to give thorough answers while being as unbiased as possible. My own thoughts as to what is best will shine through on occasion, but know that this is a serious guide to getting what you deserve, and not a glorified commercial for my company Photo Booth Plus.

As you read through the chapters of this book, we'll cover:

- The information you should know before choosing a photo booth rental company
- The questions you should ask to make sure a particular company is right for you
- What equipment will generate the highest quality photos, and prints
- Early warning signs to spot rip-offs
- How to squeeze the most out of your budget

CONTENTS

The Ultimate Guide To Picking A Perfect Photo Booth

MARTIN L. SMITH

....

OPEN AIR OR CURTAIN STYLE: WHICH PHOTO BOOTH KIOSK IS RIGHT FOR MY EVENT?

NOW THAT YOU'VE DECIDED you're interested in renting a photo booth, one of the most important decisions is choosing which style photo booth kiosk will best fit your event. Three booth styles are commonly offered: Traditional Sit-Down, Curtain Style and Open Air.

Traditional Sit-Down

The traditional photo booth became popular in the US in the early 1900s. It is coin operated, and generally consists of a sit down booth with a privacy curtain that fits 1-3 people. Original versions use an internal chemical darkroom to develop a strip of black & white photos in approximately 10 minutes.

Updated versions of the traditional style booth often include a digital camera, computer monitor with live view, video recording and even instant social media posting. Most new traditional style booths have built in Dye-Sublimation printers that print copies in seconds rather than minutes, and can create hundreds of completely dry, smudge proof photos between each change of supplies.

The traditional sit-down style isn't extremely popular at events because of its lack of portability, but it can still often be found at malls, arcades, bars and restaurants. The traditional style booth is well suited to long term installations.

Curtain Style

The curtain style booth is the modern portable adaptation of the traditional booth. Rather than being a heavy wooden or steel or structure, the majority of the booth is made up of the curtain, and all parts are constructed to be portable and easily set-up or broken-down in under an hour.

The curtain style booth started the photo booth event rental craze of the 2000s. It maintains the privacy of the traditional style booth and allows guests to take a series of photos, often with fun props that bring reserved guests out of their shells.

Since the majority of the curtain style booth's structure is made of fabric it can hold up to 8 guests comfortably, but often your guests will have the most fun trying to see how many people they can cram in uncomfortably! The backdrop of the image is designated by the color of the curtain (usually black).

The equipment used in a curtain style booth varies widely, but generally always features a camera, a button to start the photo process, and a printer.

Open Air

The open air style booth is the newest photo booth style, and the least traditional of the three options. It generally consists of a photo booth structure pointed at a backdrop.

The open air style borrows elements from a professional photographer's studio and from a celebrity red carpet. Everything is contained in a smaller package than a curtain or traditional booth, while often still maintaining the full functionality of the larger styles.

An open air style booth set up is the most adaptable of the three options. The set up can be condensed when space is a concern, configured for a full length vertical photo, or even set to take a wide angle shot of 15 guests.

Most companies offering an open air style booth will allow you to choose from different color or patterned backdrops, and offer personalized options, such as:

- *Green Screen*: Digitally change the backdrop by superimposing guests in a new scene
- *Step and Repeat*: Repeating logo backdrop seen at red carpet, corporate events & press conferences
- *Printed Graphic*: A full color printed backdrop often seen at tradeshows

- *No Backdrop*: The booth can be pointed at an attractive brick wall, garden, or into the room to capture the atmosphere of your event

Because an open air style photo booth can be tailored to the look and feel of your event, it's often the preferred choice of event planners.

In Summary...

Your booth choice boils down to preference. Some people don't feel they're actually using a photo booth unless they go into a structure. In this case, either the curtain style or a traditional sit-down booth is the right choice.

When you know your guests will be the life of the party and will love to have everyone see their antics, or when the style of booth isn't as important as the look and feel of the booth within the event space, the open air style is often a clear winner.

To choose which style photo booth rental is best for your event, be sure to consider the space available, whether you require standalone operation, the personality of your guests, and which style would best fit your décor.

Ask how many people will fit in the booth, and be sure to view current photos of the booth style you'll receive before making your reservation.

Traditional Sit-Down Photo Booth
- Benefits: Most likely to evoke nostalgia. Generally built securely enough to operate without an attendant. Structure can often be branded with graphics
- Drawbacks: Costly. Lacks portability.

Curtain Style Photo Booth
- Benefits: Portability. Privacy curtain adds nostalgia & encourages shy guests.
- Drawbacks: Large build can hog space or be an eyesore. Few backdrop options.

Open Air Style Photo Booth
- Benefits: Most portable and customizable. Red carpet feel can add elegance. Least space required. Open feel simultaneously entertains all guests.
- Drawbacks: Lacks privacy. Can be an attention hog, or overlooked if it blends in too well.

Tip: Be mindful that a curtain or open air style booth is generally best positioned against a wall, and all booths should be placed near a power outlet.

Tip: Don't automatically assume a company's open air style booth is smaller than a curtain structure. Many companies have adapted their curtain style booth to also work as an open air, and have similar spatial requirements for both.

Tip: Open air booth features can vary widely. Some booth operators have a minimal setup that consists of a camera on a tripod. Others have a fully functional offering with a touchscreen, live view and instant digital prints. As always, get details in contract form to make sure what you expect is what you'll receive.

Curtain Style Photo Booth

Open-Air Style Photo Booth

....

WHAT ARE THE MOST COMMON PHOTO BOOTH RIP-OFFS? HOW CAN I AVOID THEM?

O VER THE YEARS, THREE SCAMS have popped up regularly among clients that come to us after having a bad experience with another company.

Some photo booth companies won't be happy with me for sharing this information. Fortunately for you, I don't care much about building relationships with companies that do shady business. :)

Scam #1 – Bait & Switch

The basic principle behind the Photo Booth Bait & Switch scam is that you see an advertisement for an unbelievably low price and rush to pay and reserve the booth before the expiration date. The price is 50%-90% cheaper than the going rate, but once you've booked, you find either the package you paid for isn't compatible, or isn't offered on the day of your event.

The promise of a low price got you to pay the non-refundable deposit, and the artificially low price distracted you from making your decision based on the quality of the booth, package options, photos and service.

Bait & Switch is most commonly used along with Daily Deal sites such as Groupon or Living Social. Not every photo booth rental deal from those sites is fraudulent, but if you check for unsatisfied customer comments on closed photo booth deals, you'll see it happens fairly often.

Understanding a bit more about how deal sites work will help you spot this scheme. Daily Deal sites require a vendor to offer 50-90% off their original prices, and the deal site generally keeps half of the final discounted price charged.

To compensate for the profits lost, some photo booth companies will create a cheap package to lock you into a non-refundable agreement. Then, once your deposit is received, they tell you that the selected package won't work, but your deposit can be applied toward one of their more expensive options.

BAIT & SWITCH: WATCH OUT FOR
- Daily Deal site offers
- Prices that seem too good to be true
- Any offer you must secure with immediate payment prior to receiving full documentation
- Day of the week clauses, i.e. "You must book for at least 6 hours on Fridays or Saturdays", but you aren't made aware of that until after you've already put your deposit down on a 2 hour booth

- Deals that don't give much description of what's included

HOW TO AVOID GETTING BAIT & SWITCHED

Use search engines to research the company you're planning on booking with. See if there are negative reviews from customers who were scammed. Also, ask to see the final photo booth rental agreement in contract form before paying for anything. This document should include an itemized list of your booth's features and the payment schedule. Make sure all of the key features and benefits you expect to receive are listed on the contract. If there is a 4 hour package on the daily deal site, don't assume it includes all of the features of the 4 hour package on the company's website. In fact, don't assume anything and get everything in writing!

Scam #2 – Hidden Charges and Fees

The hidden charges scam is very similar to the Bait & Switch, since both scams show you a low price to get you interested and then ultimately end up costing you much more time and money than you initially expected.

The hidden charges scam differs in that the booth rental company isn't offering you a different rental option, they're just tacking on extra charges to increase the cost after you've already committed.

HIDDEN CHARGES AND FEES: WATCH OUT FOR

- Set up & break down costs, delivery fees & service charges added to pad the final total

- Important features that you assumed were included, that you're charged extra for once you put down your non-refundable deposit
  - » You'd like to rent the booth on a weekend? Oh, you're required to have X amount of hours...
  - » You wanted the photo booth to print photos? Ahh, that's an additional fee of...
  - » You want to access the digital photos after the event? Hmm, that will cost an extra...
- Unlisted prices and poorly described package details
- Fine print describing any additional or circumstantial fees

HOW TO AVOID HIDDEN CHARGES AND FEES

The process for avoiding this scam is the same as for a bait & switch. Do some search engine research to see if you can find negative comments or reviews. Unhappy customers tend to be extremely vocal. Request a copy of the final rental agreement. This should include a list of your booth's features as well as all of the services (set-up/breakdown) and times that things will occur. It should also include the total payment amount with all taxes and fees and when payments are due. Read any fine print carefully!

Scam #3 – The Disappearing Company

According to Bloomberg, 8 out of 10 entrepreneurs who start businesses fail within the first 18 months. Photo Booth companies are no exception to this statistic.

Clients regularly come to us after having difficulty getting in touch with the company they reserved for their event.

When a photo booth rental company goes out of business, they are often no longer accessible via the business phone number, email address or website that you were provided.

One couple contacted us the week of their wedding desperately looking for a photo booth for that Saturday. The company they originally booked only had one photo booth that was destroyed in a car accident. At the time we had 9 booths, but we were already booked solid on their date.

The disappearing company isn't always a scam, but it's no less discomforting to learn that neither a photo booth, nor the money you paid is available on the week of your event.

HOW TO AVOID THE DISAPPEARING COMPANY

You can't prevent a company from disappearing, but you can do your research. Find out if the company has a track record of happy customers. How long has the company been doing business? How comfortable do you feel that the company will still be around when it's time for your event? Do you feel secure that you could contact someone from the company even if their business closed?

These questions will help you avoid being scammed by a disappearing company:

- Do warnings or bad reviews pop up on search engines?
- Are the photos on the website generic stock photography or from the company's events?
- Are members of the company active or known in your community? That will make it easier to track them down if you ever need answers.
- Are there reviews on third party websites? It's harder to fake reviews over time on third party sites.
- Does (or did) the company have a physical office? A physical office generally means a more established company. Even if the office closes, you can contact the owner of the building to try and track down the leaseholder
- Have other vendors heard of the photo booth rental company you're hiring? If nobody else you speak to knows about the company you plan to hire, that might be cause for concern.
- Does the company have insurance? A reputable company will have liability and asset protection insurance.

THREE - BOOTH DIFFERENCES

....

HOW IS ONE PHOTO BOOTH
DIFFERENT FROM ANOTHER?

WHAT YOU CAN'T SEE CAN HURT YOU when it comes to renting a photo booth. The equipment under the hood directly affects the photo quality, print quality, speed and the overall enjoyment of using the photo booth.

The photos from the camera are passed on to the computer, processed, formed into your finished images and sent to the printer.

A weak link anywhere in this chain can dramatically affect your photo booth rental experience, so let's take some time to review the equipment options available, and see how they can affect your event.

The Camera

The first link in the photo booth chain is the camera. Options for photo booth companies range from low end webcams to high end (and high priced) DSLRs. Any of these cameras can work in a photo booth setup, but the quality increases as the camera type moves up the spectrum.

The consumer camera industry has led us to believe that more megapixels means more quality in our images. It's partially true that a camera with more megapixels can deliver higher quality images, but the quality of those pixels is more important than the quantity.

In reality, the reason that quality increases from left to right on the spectrum (seen on the next page) isn't due to megapixels, it's due to the growing image sensor size. A larger image sensor can accurately capture more detail.

The sensor in a DSLR (Digital Single Lens Reflex) is often 25 times the size of the image sensor in a point and shoot camera. Having a camera with a larger image sensor is much more important to photo quality than a camera boasting many megapixels.

DSLR cameras are the clear winner when it comes to image quality and speed. Canon and Nikon are the main brands of DSLR used by photo booth companies, and DSLR cameras from both brands produce breathtaking images. Just before DSLRs on the quality spectrum are compact Point and Shoot cameras such as the Canon SX50 that copy the DSLR size and shape but don't offer the same speed or image quality.

Cameras toward the lower end of the spectrum offer low cost and the smallest size. An iPad is a camera, computer and a touchscreen in an extremely sleek package, but the image quality of a booth that uses an iPad will be far less than the quality of a booth that uses a DSLR.

A photo booth rental company that uses a camera on the lower end of the quality spectrum may charge lower prices to compensate for the loss in image quality.

The Lighting

Next to camera quality, lighting is the most important factor in capturing a great image. Professional photo booth companies often use self-contained studio flash units to light their photos. Lower end companies often use consumer grade florescent or incandescent bulbs, which are preferable to darkness, but often produce harsh unflattering shadows characteristic of amateur photography.

CAMERA QUALITY SPECTRUM:
Webcam :: iPad :: Point & Shoot :: Compact :: DSLR

Questions to Ask: The Camera

Do you use a DSLR camera? If the answer is no, ask "Why not?" and decide if you like the answer you receive. Also ask to see various images from different events. Most professional photographers and photo booth companies own a DSLR camera, but few have mastered adjusting the settings to create appealing photographs in different environments.

Photobooth vs. Photographer

One of the questions we're asked regularly by people considering renting a photo booth is, 'Why do I need a photo booth when I have a photographer?'

A photographer captures the essence of your event, along with a healthy dose of the photographer's experience and vision.

A photo booth is an entertainment experience that generates a memorable keepsake. Preparing for the moment when the camera will snap and the instant gratification of seeing and sharing your photos are both integral parts of the photo booth experience.

Some photographers offer an open air portrait station where the photographer operates the camera as people pose in front of a backdrop. The photographer's experience means this set-up is likely to yield extremely high quality photos but it technically isn't a photo booth, because the photographer is controlling the process and there usually isn't instant access to the photos in printed or digital format.

The photo booth experience is heightened by any feature that empowers booth users to have more control over the process. For this reason, some photographer set-ups have been made more like a photo booth by adding a release button for the camera, so one of the guests can trigger the photo.

With a contemporary digital photo booth, the photo session is generally started using a button, or a touch screen, and the process includes a countdown so all guests know when the photo will be taken and can prepare their poses or props.

There's no right or wrong choice as to which operations style is best, as long as you are comfortable with the features and the amount of control your guests have over the experience.

The Computer

We're using the term 'computer' here broadly to include the overall set-up of the booth's electronics including the computer, software and monitor.

The speed and reliability of the computer and booth software directly affects the photo booth experience, but it's difficult to give guidelines for what brand, model or type of computer will be best. Even two of the exact same computers may have various software and hardware upgrades that greatly effect ultimate performance. As a customer it's less important to know about exactly which computer components and software are being used, and more important to know how the booth experience is affected by the company's computer system choice.

To gauge the computer's performance, ask the company how long it takes for a photo booth session to print once guests are done taking each set of photos? This will depend on the speed of the printer, but also on the speed of the computer. Also, look for third party reviews (beyond the company's website) to see if there is praise of fast, high quality booths or complaints of booths with poor or slow operation.

The Monitor

A monitor is one of the most useful upgrades to a photo booth setup. The monitor can be used to give instructions, show a countdown to when the photo will be taken, or to add additional customization to the booth experience, making your booth fit with the overall theme of your event.

If the booth software is live-view capable, users see a live representation of what the camera will capture. Live view is helpful to adjust outfits and props, and make sure that all guests are properly within the frame.

Having a touchscreen enabled monitor also allows the addition of interactive features like sending photos to email or social media networks.

Some older booths don't have a monitor, but instead a digital LED readout with a countdown. The guest presses a button and the digital screen shows the countdown to each photo being taken.

Having a countdown is generally preferable to not having one, but if you're interested in having a live view, make sure you ask if it's available.

The Printer

When it comes to selecting a photo booth printer there are two main options to choose from: Dye-Sublimation (Dye-Sub) or Ink-Jet.

Dye-Sub printers fuse dye from a ribbon onto paper which is then coated by a clear protective layer that resists smudges and scratches. Dye-Subs are praised for their continuous tone that closely resembles that of darkroom exposed photos.

Ink Jet printers are created by spraying tiny dots of ink on paper. Early Ink Jet models were criticized because they could not replicate the quality of color available from a Dye-Sub and you could often see visible dots and pixilation in some areas of the print. Certain brands of Ink Jet prints require drying time to avoid smudges, and can fade in sunlight if the right combination of archival ink and paper is not used.

Professional Ink Jet models have overcome many of the issues above. They use more shades of ink to create a wider color range, and have extremely tiny dots that aren't visible without magnification. With the right ink and paper choices the prints can be smudge free and last for years.

Most photo booth rental companies with Ink Jets use consumer, not professional models, which print with good photo quality but often have durability issues.

If you have the perfect combination of a professional printer, archival ink and archival paper, Ink Jet prints can look better than anything else on the market.

Ink Jet printers can use different sized sheets of paper which means photo booth strips can be larger than 2x6". A more common size for Ink Jet strips is 2x8" because the strips are cut from 8x10" photo paper. If you are offered a photo strip that is larger than 2x6" it's generally from an Ink Jet printer. Ink Jet printers are far better than Dye-Subs for reproducing small detail in text and logos.

However, Ink Jet printers print relatively slowly (30 seconds to 2 minutes per print) in comparison to Dye-Subs. Ink Jet images may smudge or fade with time. Ink Jet cartridges run out one at a time, so during the course of your event prints may have streaks or missing colors until the cartridge is replaced. The changing of cartridges may result in downtime at your event.

Dye-Sub printer quality most resembles darkroom developed photos. Professional grade Dye-Subs are generally used by photo booth companies (as well professional photo print labs) because of their extreme speed and print capacity. If the ribbon and ink needs to be changed, it will usually only be once per event. Dye-Sub prints don't suffer from smudging or fading like Ink Jets can. Although the paper size is limited, most people are used to the standard sized 2x6" strips and 4x6" photos.

The disadvantages for Dye Sub printers are that the page size and selection is limited to standard sizes. Dye Sub printers will have trouble reproducing small text and intricate logo detail if they are sized smaller than the printer can handle. High end professional Ink Jet printers offer a wider color range than Dye Subs.

The bottom line is that most professional photo booth companies use Dye Sub printers, because they offer industry standard photo quality, and are fast and reliable. You may save money by going with a company that uses consumer grade Ink Jet printers, however that cost savings can be a gamble on the quality and durability of the prints.

The Real Question

The real question that I'm sure you're already thinking: How will the advantages and disadvantages of each printer affect my photo booth rental?

Ink Jet

Advantages:
- Precise and sharp edges
- Multiple paper sizes available
- Can be cheaper than Dye-Sub printing
- Archival inkjets can be found that produce prints with long life
- Latest professional models offer incredible detail that exceeds most dye subs

Disadvantages:
- Often much slower than Dye-Subs
- Low end models may be blotchy or have visible dots in transition areas
- Most non-archival Ink Jet prints fade faster than Dye Sub prints
- Can smudge if not using the right combination of archival ink and paper
- Print heads sometimes clog and require cleaning or even replacement
- Photo booth companies using inkjets generally use consumer not archival professional models

Dye Sub

Advantages:

- Extremely fast, often less than 15 seconds per print
- Relatively maintenance free
- Smooth photos with no dot patterns visible, even when magnified. Most like real photographs
- Have large print capacities of 300-800 prints on each change of the paper & ribbon
- Excellent shadow detail in dark areas where some inkjets may be "blotchy"
- Prints are usually more durable and more water-proof than inkjet prints

Disadvantages:

- Low end models often smear high contrast edges making small text, charts, graphs, and line art look less defined
- Paper size and selection is limited
- If dust gets on the ribbon it can cause scratches on prints
- Dye sub printing cost is often higher than inkjet printing

Questions to Ask: The Printer

What type of printer do you use? How fast does each set of prints emerge? Will you send me samples of your print quality?

....

WHAT LIE IS COMMONLY TOLD BY JUST ABOUT EVERY PHOTO BOOTH RENTAL COMPANY?

ONE WORD USED by photo booth rental companies single-handedly misleads more customers than any other. Uncovering the lie behind the word will be significant in finding out what's different from one rental company to the next, and will help you select the best option for your event.

The deceptive practice is the use of the word:

"Unlimited"

If you ask 5 different companies, they will all say their service is unlimited, but in hiring them you are likely to get 5 different outcomes.

By not discussing what "unlimited" actually includes, you won't know exactly what you're being offered, and you may be unpleasantly surprised at your event after it's too late to make an adjustment.

There's generally some truth behind the service being unlimited, but there are also things you may think an unlimited photo booth rental should include that often aren't.

The Truth:

Contemporary digital photo booth rentals differ from booths of the past in that guests don't pay for each strip. The host of the event pays one rental fee in advance that allows guests to use the booth repeatedly over a certain period of time.

That repeated use is often the truth behind the term unlimited. Your guests are encouraged to use the booth frequently throughout the rental, and won't be turned away because they've used it already.

The Lie:

When contemporary digital photo booths first became available they were patterned after old style booths and only offered one or two strips per session.

However, with new curtain style and open air photo booths you can fit 10 or more people in a photo. One of the most requested features is instant photo reprints for each guest in the photo. Some companies include this in their unlimited offering, while others don't.

The real reason that the word "Unlimited" is deceptive is because your rental is always limited by the speed of the equipment. For any booth there is a limit to how many photos the camera, printer and photo booth computer can take and process in an hour.

High end equipment generally offers faster speed and better quality, but it can cost up to 10 times the price of low end models. This equipment cost will generally be passed on in the price you'll pay.

But, with fast equipment, your guests won't wait in line nearly as long and will get multiple opportunities to use the photo booth during the course of your rental period.

Consider a hypothetical event: Seven guests are waiting in line to use the photo booth.

- Company 1 offers a reprint for each guest, has a 2 minute booth process, and the printer can create two prints every 15 seconds.
  - » In 3 minutes, seven people have used the booth, each person has a print to keep, plus one can go in your scrapbook if you have one.
- Company 2 offers double prints, has a 3 minute booth process, and the printer can create two prints every 60 seconds.
  - » In 4 minutes, seven people have used the booth but only 2 people get to keep prints. If you have a scrapbook one of the prints will go into the book, so only one guest will have a printed photo to keep.

In the above example, if you have added a guest book and hire Company 1 all seven guests will have a print to take home within 5 minutes. If you hire Company 2, it will take 32 minutes for all seven guests to have a print to keep.

Even if Company 2 offered the upgraded feature of a print for each guest, the slower speed of their printer means it would take 7 minutes before the printer was ready to accept photos from the next session. This means much more waiting in line than with Company 1.

Now, you can see how a 6 hour 'Unlimited' photo booth might be a lesser value than a 2 hour booth from another company. Make sure you find out where the real limits are and how they will affect your event.

Tip: If you have an event with a short time frame, you might decide to go with printing a single 4x6" photo rather than photo strips, because it takes less time to shoot and print a single image than a strip of four. Although it might cost a bit more, your guests will view the full sized photo as a treasured keepsake.

FIVE - DIY PHOTO BOOTHS

....

WHY SHOULD I CONSIDER A DIY (DO IT YOURSELF) PHOTO BOOTH?

HERE ARE THE MAIN REASONS why people choose to build a DIY (Do-It-Yourself) photo booth, and some reasons why DIY might not be the best option for you.

<u>Reasons Why</u>
- Cost Effective – If you already have or can borrow the camera, computer and printing equipment necessary, a DIY photo booth can cost less than renting a booth.
- Highly Customizable – You'll have full control over every aspect of the quality, design and functionality of the components used.
- One of a Kind – Nobody else will have a booth exactly like yours

<u>Reasons Why You Shouldn't</u>
- Fewer Features – Unless cost isn't a factor in choosing to build a booth yourself, it's likely that

your DIY option will be fairly bare bones, so options such as Social Media Sharing, Green Screen & Live View may not be available.

- Time Consuming – The money you'll save will be in exchange for the time you'll spend figuring out the details. There are some great articles detailing what others have done, but hiring a photo booth rental company instantly frees you up to focus on the other details of your event.
- Unprofessional – Your DIY booth may look amateur when compared with other professional photo booths your guests have used.
- Untested – A professional Photo Booth company will have tested their system prior to your event to know that it will withstand constant use by many users.
- Printing? – With most DIY booths or Polaroid stations, it's more difficult to have a copy for yourself as well as copies for guests to keep. Also, if you set up a printer it will likely be a consumer ink jet so you'll have to deal with fading and smudging issues.

SIX - THE OPTIONS

....

WHAT CUTTING EDGE PHOTO BOOTH OPTIONS WOULD MAKE MY EVENT UNFORGETTABLE?

THESE FEATURES MAY NOT BE OFFERED by every photo booth rental company. However, you should be aware of them because they can help you personalize your event, and add that special touch that makes it unforgettable!

IDLE TIME

For most events you'd like the booth to be set up before guests arrive, but you don't want the hours you're paying for to be used up while hardly anyone is around to use the booth. Idle time is the perfect answer to this problem.

Idle time (also called idle hours) is a period where the photo booth is set up, but not actively in operation. The time is offered at a price lower than an active rental hour.

You can get the most value out of your photo booth rental, by scheduling your active hours for time when your guests are able to take full advantage of enjoying the booth.

If you add an idle hour at the beginning of your event and in the middle during dinner, you'll get the benefits of a 6 hour rental with the price of a 4 hour rental.

Idle hours are offered so you can squeeze every drop of value from your photo booth rental, so don't hesitate to ask if you can break the idle time up into half-hours, or 15 minute increments.

SOCIAL MEDIA SHARING

Your event is certain to go viral when enabled with Social Media Sharing. A social kiosk is the ultimate way to make everyone who couldn't attend jealous when they see how much fun your guests are having.

Some companies offer social sharing on the booth itself, but we encourage an external sharing kiosk for anything more than sending photos to email.

A kiosk away from the booth will make sure each guest can have plenty of time to post images to social networks like Facebook, Twitter, Pinterest or send by email and text message.

VIDEO BOOTHS

In addition to having the option to take photos, some companies have invested in booths that can also record videos with sound that are provided to you on a flash drive or DVD following the event.

The videos use the same photo booth countdown format, are generally anywhere up to 30 seconds in length, and are great for creating a visual guest book, or capturing testimonials.

An additional bonus of professional DSLR cameras is that newer models can record your guest's video footage in full High Definition quality, so it will look amazing on any screen from a cell phone to your home theater system.

PROJECTION SCREEN

Add an HD Projector and large format screen and showcase your guest's photos to the entire event in real time. It's hilarious to watch people run from the photo booth so they can catch their 15 seconds of fame on the big screen!

Most photo booth rental companies offer a small external monitor that shows guests standing outside of a curtain style booth what's going on inside. An HD projector takes this to the next level by showcasing the photo booth experience to everyone in attendance.

GREEN SCREEN

Imagine your guests superimposed on a beach, in a stadium, or driving a car... Any or all of those are possible at the same event! When you add a green screen to your photo booth rental, the green backdrop is automatically replaced in the printed photo by a pre-selected background graphic.

Companies with a sophisticated green screen setup will have a 'live view' screen where guests can position themselves in their virtual surroundings and see the backdrop graphic as if it's already been replaced in the photo.

For an extra visual effect, you can superimpose a graphic on top of the final photo including text, logos, or anything that you can dream of.

....

THE ONE QUESTION YOU MUST ASK YOUR PHOTO BOOTH COMPANY: NOT KNOWING THE ANSWER COULD RUIN YOUR EVENT?

T HERE'S ONE QUESTION YOU MUST ASK your Photo Booth rental company before signing a contract. It will give insight into how the company treats its customers, and most importantly it will prepare you for the unexpected. That question is:

What happens if something goes wrong?

Most photo booth rental companies have non-refundable deposits because booths often book up to a year or more in advance. It's often difficult to re-book if a customer were to reserve a booth only to cancel days before the event date.

Since your down payment is non-refundable, before you book you should be certain of what will happen if services can't be provided, especially, if those reasons are outside of your control.

Photo booths are made of electronic equipment, and occasionally batteries die, computers crash & printers jam. How well is the company you intend to hire prepared to handle these situations? Do they have back up equipment on hand in the case of an equipment failure? Do they have more than one booth? How have they handled these experiences in the past?

Beyond the technical difficulties of the booth, the attendant could get ill, or have a car that doesn't start. Will your money be refunded if the fault is the company's?

I recently purchased an end of season sale item from an online store. UPS lost the delivery and since it was the last one available I couldn't get a replacement. The store issued me credit, which I prefer to them saying, "Oh well, we shipped it, the rest is your problem." But, I was disappointed because I only purchased because of the deep discount. Now, I'm forced to wait until next year's sale, or buy another item at full price.

If your event is cancelled, what is the company policy? Even if the cancellation is your fault, will you at least get credit towards a future event? Will the company guarantee that you will get what you pay for? What will you get in return if you're not happy with their service?

In most areas there is no business license required to operate a photo booth, but a reputable company should at least have liability insurance if something was to hurt one of your guests. It's great if they have equipment replacement insurance too. If they have both types of insurance, you are less likely to be on the receiving end of a lawsuit, and they are more likely to be in business even if something unexpected happens prior to your event.

Tip: Check online reviews and mentions about the company to make sure that what you're being promised aligns with what previous customers have experienced.

MARTIN L. SMITH

....

12 RULES FOR RENTING A PHOTO BOOTH

DO's

DO Ask:

- How long have you been in business?
- What happens if something goes wrong?
- What equipment do you use in the booth & Why?
- Other trusted vendors if they've heard of your photo booth rental company

DO Set-Up:

- In a highly visible area
- Against a wall & near a power outlet
- An external monitor so guests are entertained in line
- In an adjacent room that can be closed off for set-up or break-down

DO Get Full Value By:
- Having your MC or DJ announce the booth (and the guest book/scrapbook if you have one)
- Seeing photos of the booth before you reserve, to make sure the type & décor fits your event
- Placing photo strip frames at guests seats encouraging photo booth use
- Including props to help guests break out of their shells

DON'Ts

DON'T Get Ripped Off:
- Do search engine research, and read all reviews
- Avoid scams by asking for a contract with full details
- Check for liability and equipment insurance
- Be very careful with Daily Deals
- Ask for a definition of 'Unlimited' Use

DON'T Set-Up Poorly By:
- Placing the booth in a low traffic area
- Putting a green screen booth across from a window: Harsh light or shadows are bad for green screen photography
- Allowing the arrival or departure time to disrupt your event (see 'Idle Time' in chapter 6)
- Assuming the booth will accommodate children, tall guests or the disabled. If any of these would be an issue, ask if the booth is adjustable

- Advise the company about the needs of your guests in advance and ask if the booth will accommodate them

DON'T Forget to Watch Out For:
- Low quality photos: Ask for examples that are not already shown on the company's web site. Owning a DSLR camera doesn't always mean you know how to operate it
- Bulky or ugly booths: Ask for photos of the company's current booth
- Fading or Smudging prints: Confirm the Printer option being used

MARTIN L. SMITH

....

THE SINGLE MOST IMPORTANT COMPONENT TO GETTING WHAT YOU DESERVE

THE SERVICE YOU RECEIVE is often the most important component to whether you have a successful event. By service, we mean the overall efforts of the photo booth rental company to make sure you're happy before, during and after your event.

As always, we suggest that you read the reviews carefully. No reviews indicate a new and possibly inexperienced company. Most companies will have reviews that say, "The booth was wonderful, everyone loved it!" However, what you're looking for is something that shows the company will go above what's generally expected to ensure you have a successful event.

The level of service is almost always linked with the price of the offering. Cut rate prices might initially seem like a win, but they are often a recipe for disaster. When the price is extremely low, that generally means the company doesn't pay employees well, so they can't attract and keep the most talented workers. There may not be enough staff to serve you promptly, and there's often little to no budget for dealing with unexpected issues.

During a particularly harsh Michigan winter, more than a foot of snow fell in one day. We had an event booked that evening. It took almost 6 hours to drive what usually takes less than an hour. We ended up paying our attendant for twice the hours she was scheduled for, and secured a hotel room so she didn't have to drive home until the next day when the snow was cleared.

Yes, we probably lost money on that event, but due to charging a fair price overall, we were able to absorb that loss, compensate our attendant, and provide great service where another company may have just called and cancelled.

There's only one way a company can show it is completely dedicated to the success of your event, and that's by having an unconditional satisfaction guarantee. Just like the length a product warranty tells you when the company expects that product to need repair, if your photo booth company does not offer a guarantee, that should tell you something about level of service it is committed to providing.

Before Your Event:

Prior to your event, you'll want to watch out for red flags that indicate you'll have a hard time getting in contact with a staff person at your photo booth company. Are phone calls and emails returned in a timely manner? Do they seem excited to work with you? Do you feel that your business is important to the company?

One of the most important things to handle before your event is personalization of your experience. A professional photo booth company should be knowledgeable about the process of customizing things for you, and helpful in making sure that your photo booth will be unique.

Often packages include the design of a custom logo. Have you seen sample work from the person that will design your logo? Ask to view examples of exactly what you should expect in terms of the logo and the quality of the photos.

<u>During Your Event:</u>

Even if you choose the perfect photo booth rental, poor service during your event can ruin the experience. We've often heard stories of attendants that were mean, or too introverted for guests to enjoy themselves. If the person you're dealing with in booking your photo booth isn't very pleasant, that might infer that the company's staff in general isn't very outgoing.

When will the booth set-up and break down occur? It generally will take 30 minutes to 2 hours for most portable photo booth systems to be transported and assembled, or broken down. Find out when that set up process will occur. Will you be charged for the set up and break down time? Will it disturb your event?

To further personalize our set-up to our client's needs we offer a service called Idle Time. That is a block of time where the booth is set up, but not in operation. It's great for weddings or other events where you'd like the booth to be set up in advance, but don't want to open the booth to your guests until you know everyone will be available.

After Your Event:

Following your event, you can usually expect to receive copies of your photos in one format or another. If you have ordered a photo guest book, you will likely get a scrapbook full of photos on the day of your event. Some companies will also provide you with a flash drive or DVD of photos on the day of, or soon after your event. Make sure you know what to expect in terms of delivery of your photos following the event.

Of course everyone hopes for a flawless event, but if this isn't the case, how will things be resolved? Do you feel comfortable that you'll be able to contact someone to resolve an issue once your event is over and the company has already been paid in full? Once again, a guarantee is a good clue that will give insight as to how reputable the company is, and whether they'll see things through from start to finish.

Here are three questions that when answered will shed light on the service you can expect:

1. Do you offer a guarantee?
2. What happens when something goes wrong?
3. When have you gone above and beyond to ensure the success of a client event?

TEN - STRETCHING YOUR BUDGET

....

HOW TO GET THE MOST FROM YOUR PHOTO BOOTH RENTAL BUDGET

THROUGHOUT THIS BOOK I've tried to be as unbiased as possible and explore all available photo booth rental options. Here, I make no apologies for being biased. If I were you, this is how I'd get the most for my money.

How Much Rental Time Do I Need?

The time you need depends on what print options you choose and the number of guests. As mentioned in previous chapters, a 2 hour booth from one company may serve the same number of guests as a 6 hour booth from another company, so there's no universal answer to this question.

However, if you're looking to save money by selecting a package with a lower number of booth hours, choose a company with fast equipment to give you the most more bang for your buck.

How Much Should I Pay?

There's no specific dollar amount you should look to pay. I suggest using this book to determine your 'must have' features and options. Then, spend the lowest amount you can, to get the photo and print quality, features, customization and service guarantees that you desire.

Insider Tips to Stretch Your Budget:

• Reserve a photo booth rental that offers a print for each guest, it will give you the lowest cost per print.

• Choose a booth with a Dye Sub printer. The print speeds will be fastest, so there will be less time spent waiting in line. Because speed is required, companies that offer a print for each guest also tend to use Dye Sub printers.

• Select a booth with a screen that has a live view. Guests will be able to visually frame themselves in the photo beforehand, so there will be fewer botched photos and retakes that hold up the line.

• Make use of Idle Hours (lower cost time where the booth is set up, but not available to guests) to ensure the booth is open during the time your guests will be most able to use it.

....

CHECKLIST: 10 QUESTIONS YOU SHOULD ALWAYS ASK BEFORE RENTING A PHOTO BOOTH

THIS 10 QUESTION CHECKLIST summarizes the information covered in this book. Before booking, ask your photo booth company these questions. The answers will make certain that you choose the right photo booth for your event, get it at the best possible price, and avoid getting ripped off in the process.

Selecting the Right Photo Booth Rental:

1. WHICH PHOTO BOOTH KIOSK STYLE IS BEST? Find out which photo booth style is best for your event. Would you prefer a traditional Curtain Style booth, a cutting edge Open-Air booth, or a classic Sit-Down photo booth? Which styles are offered by the company, and which will best fit the personality of your event and your guests?

2. WHAT QUALITY CAN I EXPECT? What type of camera, lighting, printer and computer is the company using? Why did they choose those components, and how do they affect the photo and print quality you'll receive? How many seconds will it take to print each copy? Ask to view sample photos similar to what you will receive. If lesser equipment is being used, does the price reflect this?

3. HOW 'UNLIMITED' IS YOUR PHOTO BOOTH RENTAL? Is there a limit to how much the booth can be used? How many prints are available each time guests use the photo booth? If there are limited prints available per use, does the cost reflect this?

4. HOW DO I PERSONALIZE THE EXPERIENCE? Is a custom logo, prop box, scrapbook, projection screen or social media sharing kiosk available to help your guests create lasting memories? Who will create the personalization? Have you seen samples of the quality of design work available? Will the personalization options offered help your event stand out?

5. WHAT PRINTING OPTIONS ARE AVAILABLE? The most common print sizes are 2x6" photo booth strips or 4x6" photos. Which will you receive? Will physical prints be available immediately? Will you be able to share photos instantly via social media? Will digital or printed copies of the photos be provided after your event? How long can you expect to wait before you receive them? If physical prints aren't available, does the cost reflect this?

How to Protect Yourself, and Avoid Disaster:

6. WHERE CAN I READ YOUR CUSTOMER REVIEWS? Does the company have client reviews or testimonials? The most unbiased reviews will be on 3rd party sites. Look for comments that are out of the ordinary. What are people saying about that company over and above the basic, "Photo booths are so much fun"?

7. WHAT HAPPENS WHEN SOMETHING GOES WRONG? This is the most important question to ask. You must specifically ask, "What happens if something goes wrong at my event?" How prepared are they for the unexpected? Does the company have more than one booth? Is back up equipment available? Are they insured?

8. WHAT IS YOUR GUARANTEE? Is the company willing to guarantee that your event will go successfully? No company can promise that you won't have any issues, but a solid guarantee means the risk is on the company, not on you. If there are problems, what will they do to make things right?

9. WILL YOU SEND ME EVERYTHING IN WRITING? Avoid scams. Before you pay anything, ask to see a written contract including the date, start and end time, all features and benefits you'll receive and the final price you'll pay. Are there strange fees you weren't aware of like charges for set up and break down time? Are there any additional fees on the contract that you

weren't expecting? If so, that can signal more unexpected surprises down the road.

10. ASK YOURSELF – HAVE YOU NOTICED RED FLAGS? How certain are you that you'll be able to find and contact them before, and after your event if you have questions, or if something goes wrong? Does the company seem well established? After viewing the company website, reviews, sample photos and videos, do you feel the company is reputable?

Now that you've found the perfect photo booth rental, and have avoided disaster, here's one additional question that will help maximize the experience during your event.

11. WHERE SHOULD WE SET UP THE BOOTH? Set up the photo booth where it will be highly visible, but won't disrupt the flow of traffic. Leave adequate space for a line of excited guests to queue. If your event is outside, try to place the photo booth in a covered area to protect against overpowering direct sunlight, and inclement weather. Finally, make sure there are signs for the photo booth, so guests know what the structure is and feel invited to use it.

Most importantly... HAVE FUN!

ABOUT THE AUTHOR

Martin L. Smith is co-owner of Michigan based Photo Booth Plus. Launched in 2009 as a part of Snapfuze Photo Booth & DJ Services, in 2012 extreme success prompted Martin and cofounder Andrew Yim to spin the popular booths off into their own company.

Since it's inception, Photo Booth Plus has remained at the forefront of the industry serving private events, and leveraging its social media integration to become the go-to company for high profile corporate & celebrity events.

www.ingramcontent.com/pod-product-compliance
Lightning Source LLC
Chambersburg PA
CBHW060641280326
41933CB00012B/2102